MIND OF A MADAM

MY THOUGHTS AND POEMS

ERYKA EDWARDS

ACKNOWLEDGMENT

I thank GOD for revealing and rebirthing this purpose-driven poetry. I thank GOD for allowing me to have the courage, so I may deliver myself to the world to help others. I know I have more work to do in this world and this is only the beginning. I want to thank GOD for allowing me to finish what I started, another way for HIM to help heal others.

CONTENTS

CONTENTS

CONTENTS

CONTENTS

CONTENTS

MATTERS OF A MADAM

OUT OF ALL THE JOBS I HAD, I LOVED YOU THE MOST

I LOVED YOU SO MUCH, I MUST SAY I LIKE TO BOAST

YOU GIVE ME FREEDOM, LIFE, AND UNDERSTANDING

WITH THIS JOB IT'S NOT SO DEMANDING

I CAN FREE MY MIND AND GIVE THE WORLD MY THOUGHTS

I CAN STAY UP LATE IT'S WORTH PAYING THE COST

I KNOW IN THE END I WILL FEEL SO FULFILLED

IM DOING GODS WORK AND ITS ALL IN HIS WILL

FULFILLING MY PURPOSE TO SCRATCH THE SURFACE IS ALL I WANT TO
DO

TO POUR OUT MY HEART AND GIVE THESE BEAUTIFUL POEMS TO ALL
OF YOU

THERE IS NO LIMIT HOW FAR I CAN GO, I HAVE SO MUCH INSIDE

COME AND WALK THROUGH MY DOOR

I WILL POUR OUT MY EXPERIENCES, FOR THERE IS NOTHING TO HIDE

SO SIT BACK, LAUGH, AND SAY OH MY OH MY

FOR THIS IS WHO I AM, THE BOOK OF THE MATTERS OF A MADAM

EE

Anywhere I Want to Be

I want some where I can grow that gives me energy down in my soul

I want to feel it down in the marrow of my bones

I want to be somewhere to be free and be who I want to be

I want to go where the wind blows

I want to be gravitated by love songs that say here is where you belong

I want to be where there are pretty palm trees hovering over top of me

I want to wear grace like a cloak of a superhero in the streets

I want to hit the stage and be amazed at how the fans gaze when the lights hit my face

So I can speak these words in my poems to take me somewhere that keeps my heart warm in the sun

For it gives me life to celebrate myself

Be the reason to celebrate myself because it takes me somewhere else

Anywhere I want to be free by my poetry

EE

I HEAR YOU

WHISPERS OF MY MAJESTY SPEAKING IN MY EAR

SOFT WORDS OF DIRECTION IT HAD TO BE CLEAR

IF IT WASN'T FOR HIS LOVE AND GRACE, I WOULD BE LEFT WITH NO
CHEER

THE LOVE THAT HE GIVES TO ME, I HAVE TO KEEP HIM NEAR

THE WONDEROUS WIND BLOWS AS I WALK WITH HIM

AS HE SPEAKS TO THE SWEET BIRDS I HEAR THEM IN MY EAR

REMINDING ME THAT HES NEVER TO FAR FROM ME

FOR I AM FREE TO BE TOTALLY FREE AND HAPPY

NO NEED TO BE UNHAPPY BECAUSE HE IS ALWAYS WITH ME

EE

On Paper

No one knew I had it in me

I write on paper what my mind and eyes could see

Life reflections of me

I am going to write for the rest of my days

I'm going to write while drinking fresh-squeezed lemonade in the shade

This Scorpio characteristic has me feeling pretty optimistic

I feel I'm in my element

Being bold and writing from my soul

Writing makes me feel like I'm in control

Writing makes me feel whole

Come to get a dose of my life exposed

EE

BECAUSE OF YOU

I TRY TO CONVINCE MYSELF THAT THE ONLY REASON WHY I WANT YOU SO MUCH IS BECAUSE I CAN'T HAVE YOU.

MY ONLY REASON FOR PUTTING PENCIL TO PAPER IS FOR THE THOUGHT OF YOU.

A CONSTANT THOUGHT, ME WISHING I FELT MY FINGERTIPS TOUCHING THE SOFTNESS OF YOUR SKIN.

WANTING TO EXHALE LOOKING AT THE HANDSOME BECOMING OF YOUR FACE.

THOUGHTS OF CONVERSTATIONS ENHANCES MY ENTER THOUGHTS, MAKING ME HAVE THE INSIDE DESIRE FOR WORDS.

THE ACTURAL PERSONALITY MAKES ME WANT TO EXPAND MY MIND TO LOVE AGAIN.

THE UNINVITED SEXUAL THOUGHT GIVES ME THE DESIRE TO WANT TO EXPLORE THE MIND, BODY, AND SOUL TO EXTASY.

THEY SAY THE MIND IS A TERRIBLE THING TO WASTE, I SAY THE DESIRE FOR THOUGHTS LEAVES A MIND WASTEFUL.

THAT'S WHY MY THOUGHTS HAS THE DESIRE TO LOVE ONCE AGAIN.

EE

Dear Daddy

I knew you were him the first moment I laid eyes on you

And you never acted as if you had no clue

Even though you denied me being your child

Thought I was a white man's baby for a long while

Even still I admired your beautiful radiant smile

That Indian nose of mine gave it away as a child

The love between us is undeniable, but you still refused to take responsibility is unjustifiable

Moms told me how you beat and kick her in the belly, knowing I was inside of her you could have caught a felly

But still my love never changes; for sure I'm a daddy's girl with hope for tomorrow to be born into this world without any sorrow

Waiting on you one day just to show up, not just with a hundred dollars, but for you to own up to be your baby's father

Instead you let another man take your place, but still your face in my mind I could not erase

He only came by when it was convenient for him, I had two daddies baby but what's the reason slims

My mom pushed me hard to get that money for her, from both of my daddies only to give her dollars she didn't deserve

I wonder if it's because you both were raised by others, that has hopped onto me unfortunately like most others

History tells it all because you left no legacy, haunted by your thoughts of the death penalty

The rumors I've heard you have more than me, where's my sister now does she look like me

Caught up in that guilt and that loneliness while your daughter sit around in this good ole holiness

That liquor got you bound in the world of forgetfulness, that addiction had you gone living a life of carelessness

That phone call of those cries asking for forgiveness, I mean really all I wanted is just for you to listen

Promises of a red Mustang when I turned sixteen, the best thing is to go buy a candy apple red mustang figurine

Father's relationships are important so you won't go stray, without a solid mother I really needed you to stay

As I got older I didn't care much anymore, Fathers lost time it does not pay much only ten times over

Still loved you to death and still do to this day, we look just a like I mean what can I say

Now I am an adult I still offered to take care of you because a real daughter's loves who will still see you through

I even changed my last name to honor you, inside I grew, I understood the situation but you had no clue

Honor thy father and you days will be longer, in this life without a physical Father only made me stronger

God is my father at the end of each day, no worries dad I was well-taking care of in every way

EE

7

I LOST MY APETITE FOR YOU

ALL MY LIFE I'VE WANTED AND WAITED ON YOU

I LOVED AND HONORED YOU

I BELIEVED AND COUNTED ON YOU

BUT I WAS NEVER ENOUGH, NEVER ENOUGH

ALL MY LIFE I ADORED YOU AND THANKED GOD FOR YOU

I FELT FOR YOU AND VIBED WITH YOU

I WANTED MORE FROM YOU AND FELT YOU WERE TRUE

BUT I WAS NEVER ENOUGH, NEVER ENOUGH

ALL MY LIFE I DESIRED YOU, EVEN IN YOUR DECISIONS, I SIDED WITH
YOU

I COULDN'T BELIEVE HOW I FELL FOR YOU AND WOULD RIDE FOR
YOU

BUT I WAS NEVER ENOUGH, NEVER ENOUGH

ALL THIS TIME I WAISTED AND NOW I KNOW, YOU WERE NEVER
ENOUGH, NEVER ENOUGH

I WAS ONLY TO MUCH, ONLY TO MUCH FOR YOU

AND NOW I HAVE LOST MY APETITE FOR YOU

EE

JESUS, JESUS, JESUS

When they would haunt me in my dreams and I would wake up in screams

My mother always told me to call out Jesus, Jesus, Jesus

When they hold me down and had me bound

My mother always told me to call out Jesus, Jesus, Jesus

When they had me scared, I put the covers over my head

My mother always told me to call out Jesus, Jesus, Jesus

When I had those out of body experiences felt like I was levitating

I would call out Jesus, Jesus, Jesus

When I felt that unforgettable breeze in my sleep

I would fall to my knees and call out Jesus, Jesus, Jesus

My mother always told me that God would always protect me

All I needed to do is call out Jesus, Jesus, Jesus

The most Powerful name I know is Jesus

EE

LET ME STEW LIKE SOUP

I FELT AS THOUGH I COULD NOT MOVE FROM YOU.

I COULD LAY THERE FOREVER AND STEW LIKE SOUP.

NOTHING EVEN MATTERS, FOR I WAS IN THE SHADE.

I KNEW I COULDN'T SLEEP IT AWAY BUT WANTED TO LAY AND JUST MARINATE.

WHEN THAT STAR CALLED, IT PUT A LITTLE SUNSHINE IN MY DAYS.

I CAME OUT FROM AMOUNGST THE DARK INTO THE LIGHT, KIND OF WANTING TO RETURN AGAIN.

THIS FEELING HAS TAKEN OVER ME, FOR I KNOW THIS HAS TO BE A SIN.

LORD FORGIVE ME FOR WHAT HAS TAKEN PLACE WITHIN.

FOR ALL I WANT IS FOR ALL THESE SAD STORIES TO END.

THIS APPETITE FOR LOVE HAS ME NEVER WANTING TO TRY IT AGAIN.

EE

MaDukes

I have so many MaDukes in this World

What can Women do with so many Mommas, you're like endless pearls

I am privileged, blessed, and grateful I don't want to share

I love them to the bone, Iddy Clare

Even when I call them MaDukes, I can feel us both smile

The love is always felt even if we haven't spoken for a while

I would never be without a Maduke because I have so many

I know if I didn't have much their love was aplenty

I thank God for them all because they warm my soul

They're like a warm bowl of soup in the winters cold

I don't know what I would do without them, but it feels good to know your there

Your love is masterpiece better than art I Clare

I admire and adore you no matter where I go

You're my true soul tie, just like a piece of warm apple pie

EE

Ms. Genuine

I've been admired by most but valued by few

She sees me with you, watching me but wanting you

Not realizing, I am God made that's why I look the way that I do

Classy, fierce, and wonderfully made, yea this is true

My style is so immaculate to bad your life is a cascade

I am an ocean; my dopiness is in my DNA

Breed by MBM, led by God

In this life I was meant to go hard, I am my own squad

Only the strong will survive, fleshed bind, overcome by the beauty of the eye

My presence is felt; with no surprise, I light up the room

They told me so, but I don't have to assume

It's the God in me, my love is felt when I walk through the door

Like a Gisele with an eloquent pose

I stay genuine from the heart, my blood stay pumping through my pores

My cousin always told me there's no future in fronting

Once you acknowledge my energy, it will leave your mind wanting

It's a known fact that my energy is just calming

Constantly on your mind even when you find time to unwind

Just have me as a friend and call me Miss. Genuine

My So-Called Friends

He left me for my so-called friend, one who rode off in the Benz for all he could see is through his Versace lenses.

You and my so-called friend laughed and set back and smoked with bottles of Mo.

He left me for my so-called friend, the friend at that wedding where it all begins.

Starting acting funny when it was all over nothing, now you're left with only making money

When I left you all for my so-called friends it doesn't mean what you think

I had to leave you all to let it sink in

You left me for my so-called friends that weren't solid to begin

Now we are all separated in the end

I knew you all were shady to begin

The hidden agenda and secrets behind my back

Some wonder why it even would be a thought to take you back

No love lost for I am willing to forgive

For God spares grace and mercy

And I have to forgive to live

EE

My Wet Wuzzle Whistles

My Wet Wuzzle Whistles in this dry season.

You say I'm in the situation for no solid reason.

I'm waiting for the day to exhale.

Take a boat that will sail to find that holy grail.

Send me away in the ocean and I will fall in love with the motion.

With the possibility of rain, strong currents at the sea.

But at least I'll be where God wants me to be.

He says peace be still.

My Wet Wuzzle Whistle will not matter, He makes me whole again.

For I will be his beloved one without that fleshy sin.

EE

The Energy of God

One day, I was complaining to myself that the love of my life was doing things that made me feel a little uncomfortable. I was to the point of distancing myself from him. In my mind, I kept hearing this voice saying, "Look around you." I kept thinking to myself what does that mean. As I was sitting there contemplating about what was I planning on doing. I heard the voice again, "Look around you." The voice repeatedly said it over and over again. Until I stop thinking about the situation. I started thinking about what was spoken to me. Even though it had taken a while for me to understand what was going on, I finally started looking around. As I was looking around, I started thinking, look what God has done for me. Look where he has bought me from. I begin to smile and my energy immediately changed. I say that to say, before we start spending our energy wonder, worrying, waiting, and complaining about anything, be sure to look around you and focus on what matters, "The energy of God."

EE

The Solution to Love

In relationships they tend to grow old at times, things happen, or you don't know what else to do. We tend to run out of the things to say or just feel as if we need to go our separate ways. Would you say it was true love if you hold on? Would you stay because of the children? Would you stay because it's the right thing to do? We all have so many minds irritating thoughts about what should I do? Should I stay or should I go? Sometimes we don't ever really know. Afterward, when it's over, we ask ourselves did I make the best choice. Or this is the best choice I could have ever made! Sometimes life and love just don't mix. Sometimes you can't get anything done because loves is in the way. How do we separate the two? How do we love and live? Do we have a life like Will and Jada? One of those relationships that we understand we are human and every man and women have needs. Or as long as we have respect and understand each other. Relationships, marriages, arrangements, and whatever else there is. Make the best of it, if it's not working make the end of it. It's ok to be alone if that's what's best for you. Don't let the relationship take your life because God gave it to you. The true essence of love comes from within. If God doesn't live within you then you should try him first. Love will never work if God is not first. For, God is love, he will help you live, and putting all this together will make it seal.

EE

Different Type of Appetite

All I ever wanted was solid friends, with a glass wine, good conversation, and sweet cigars.

I ask for nothing more, nothing less.

Honestly, I'm really tired of the mess.

Wrongful communication, insensitive insinuations, backward obligations.

The mindset of many is not what I ask for, not what I paid for, and not what I deserve.

I realize that I'm on another level that is just unheard.

No one is listening because they think their way is right.

I'm here to tell you, to indulge in this different type of appetite with a glass wine, good conversation, and sweet cigars.

Nothing more, nothing less just be a solid friend and without a bunch of mess.

EE

You Know How We Do

My cousin is so dope; she is the realest person I know

She taught me there is no future in fronting; just follow your soul and go

To set goals and focus on getting this money don't get distracted by people unless you'll end up a dummy

Don't let people control you, for no one has dominion over you,

Make sure you put God first through the windows of your eyes

They will tell the story of what's going on in your life

Make sure life is good and you're understood, that this paper is always good

Yes money can be the root of all evil but if you use it wisely it won't be an equal

She told me that I would always have problems with Women and their mouth will be poked out like they tasted lemons

The beauty on the outside they wouldn't understand that the beauty on the inside is always in demand

Stand strong and make things happen don't procrastinate

Time waits for no man

Make sure you have your own roof over your head

Make sure you're fed and gain knowledge of that leavened bread

I would not trade her for the world; she has stood by me since I was a little girl

No matter the situation she always gives it to me real

She's always had my back and made sure I knew what the deal

I would give her my last and she would do the same for me because love is more than a dollar, hell it's free

We have this saying "you know how we do" and it is true that is how we do

EE

You Remind Me

You remind of the life that was never intended for me

You remind me of project open doors, that smells clean but dirty Clorox floors

You remind me of old cold houses with tin roofs, and cement porches

You remind me of unwanted trash onside of the road and ramped roaches

You remind me of poor people, crack heads, and alcoholics

A woman that was never much of a workaholic

You remind me of neighborhood candy and liquor houses

The plastic cover on those ugly couches

You remind me of old buildings, damp floors, and liquor stores

Go pick up that booze, you have to get some more

You remind me of filthy debris on the side of the streets

Filled up street side trashed cans and perverted Mexicans

The pimping pushing mom for both daddies' hands

You remind of mildew sour laundry, clutter house that smells funny

Packrat for that insanity, holding on to things that give off energy

You remind me of greasy foods that have you sick for days

Food that's not right that will take you to your grave

You remind me of voodoo, death, and that unrighteousness

Doing evil in the dark with that spitefulness

Most people love you, hate you, or right in between

You don't play any games when you come on the scene

Energy is so sweet if you know what I mean

You clean up well; it's so hard to tell

Nothing really good from back in the day

Thank God I wasn't raised around you and was given away

Thoughts of suicide I'm sure would have been in play

I pray that you have changed with no evil inside

My love for you, unfortunately, I cannot hide

I pray for a Purified heart asking God to forgive

To live a better life so you're able to live

In peace, love, harmony, and know that I love you still

You remind me of my mom that I once knew

God has a way of making all things new

EE

I Still Loved You

I remember the times I would see you and I knew it wasn't you

I saw the evil demon that took over you, but I still loved you

Saying to myself he is someone else, but I still loved you

I remember you would eat as though you could not get enough

You were not as clean, you didn't smell like you, but I still loved you

You would hang around others just like you, but I still loved you

At times I felt I needed you even though you weren't around but I still loved you

Even when you went away and I missed your smile I still loved you

I remember when you would knock on my window and cry to let you in

Awaken out of my sleep, afraid, but not afraid because I still loved you

In spite of my nightmares, that wouldn't go away I still loved you

I knew I would get in trouble if I let you in but I didn't care because I stilled loved you

No matter what you did that caused chaos I still loved you

No matter the cost, I still loved you

No matter how much I worried and prayed for you to be ok, I still loved you

No matter the state that my Brother was in I still loved him

No matter what I saw that demon within him, I still loved him

I knew my brother was in the inside because he never tried to hurt me

I knew my Sister was afraid even though she didn't show it but I was unafraid because I knew you still loved me

Nothing else mattered at the end of the day, a Brother and Sister love will never fade away

EE

Going Somewhere

I hide behind my smile with that rainy mist of misery blown away in the cloud

Look up into the sky and seeing the clouds of Heaven gates open with all sorts of wonders

Reminds me of blue and pink soft baby colors

For it only comes and goes as I feel the wind blow

This Hawaii weather helps the love left flow

As I exhale this air feels like I lost my every breath in time

I sit back and try to relax as I have so many thoughts going through my mind

Should I stay should or should I go, if I was younger I would just smoke some dro

But these trees hovering over me are protecting me from the NO

I have to dive deep to find me, the depths of the ocean of my soul

I come up through these life waves then sink back down in the ocean hole

The rainbow continuously confirms His promises. I surrender to you God for you are my true Master

This transformation you have me going through, it has me feeling like a weather forecaster

As I look up in the deep dark blue and Gods bright stars look down, wink, and smile to say I love you

And up there the moon reminds me that even in the darkest places there still is light too

The darkness where I find peace in my sleep every night

This next move I make will be on the next flight…

EE

My Prayers Somedays

My Father, It's hard to mass the devastating pain that's all over me

Some days I feel like I'm going insane because it's all over me

Having outburst of tears from within, spilling on the outside me

I ask forgiveness some days because I know you see me

I feel I'm locked in a box and I have no escape

Not knowing what to do just asking God to help me to carry this weight

I need strength Lord like I never needed it before

This love has me trapped like there are no open doors

I need you Father, I feel I'm at the very end

All I have been trying to do is have faith within

Living every day without speaking any words

Praying in my head and communing with the birds

Knowing what I desire and what I deserve

I'm a Child of God, I guess he hasn't really heard

Some days it seems he cares, some days in his presence I feel I don't exist

Some days it seems like I'm at the bottom of his list

As my heart keeps crumbling away and trying to survive the day to day

I have these crazy headaches praying to God to take them away

As I succumb to the crazy thoughts, I focus on my godliness

My God will supply all my needs for that is what he promises

It Is Still A Queens Way

It is hard being in a place and feels like he does not want me, desire me, or needs me

Grieving is like 8-day old leftovers that almost spoiled, screaming it's no good for me

Like old bread on the edge ready to mold, I feel like he has taken half of my soul

Some day's I'm good, some days I'm all in my head, some days I just want to lay in bed

All it takes is one thing to trigger that madness, and then here comes the sadness

This pain has to stop I can't take it anymore; I wish I had the money to walk right out the door

Trying to make the best out of this unbelievable situation, trying to get away from this love aggravation

It may be the best opportunity because I don't carry any weight, kids, just little ole me

I don't know where to go because my eyes cannot see. I try to tell myself just let it be

I feel like I'm stuck in a box with some old stale funky socks

Living in this mundane world and still in shock

Releasing me from wasn't my reality

Walking around drinking chamomile and lavender herbal tea

Coming here believing sin would be at the end, this is so orthodox

Everything happens for a reason and I thank my Father for it now watch the next 365 day of my life orbit

Victory is always mine at the end of the day. I leave with no conflict because that's the Queen's way

EE

<u>Move On</u>

Nothing you can do when it's not how you imagined it to be.

You have to accept it and move accordingly.

EE

THE BEAUTY IN SKY

AT MIDNIGHT I WISH THE SKY COULD TURN UPSIDE DOWN, SO I COULD WALK IN THE COLOR OF MIDNIGHT.

MAKE IT WARM LIKE THE SUN ON A SUNDAY BEACH DAY WHEN IM HAVING FUN.

I WISH I COULD GO UP TO THE MOON AND OPEN UP A CRATER IN YOU AND PEAK ALL THE WAY THROUGH TO THE OTHERSIDE TO SAY I LOVE YOU.

I WISH I COULD TAKE MY FINGER AND HIT THE TIP OF A STAR AND MAKE IT SPIN LIKE A SPIN WHEEL.

PLAY AROUND IN THE SKY TO LET IT KNOW I APPRECIATE WHAT YOU GIVE TO ME.

YOUR BEAUTY EXCITES ME.

EE

MEET ME IN MY DREAMS

WHEN I CLOSE MY EYES

I SEE BLANK SPACES

WHERE THERE ARE NO FACES

THERE'S WHERE I FEEL THE SAFEST

I SLEEP SO PEACEFULLY

EE

GIVE HIM WHAT YOU OWE

YOU SHOULD NEVER DELAY IN GOD'S PAY.

PAY HIM WHAT YOU OWE HIM THAT'S 10% OUT EACH DOLLAR.

AS MUCH AS GOD GIVES ME; ONE BEING LIFE ALONE.

HOW CAN I NOT GIVE BACK TO HIM.

AS MUCH AS I HAVE GIVEN TO OTHERS, NEVER GOT IT BACK OR
WANTED ANYTHING IN RETURN.

SOME DIDN'T EVEN DESERVE IT.

I HESITATE WITH PEOPLE, BUT NOT WITH MY TITHING WITH GOD.

EE

THE BACK IN THE DAY

I LOOK AROUND, HAWAII REMINDS ME OF THE BACK IN THE DAY

IT REMINDS ME OF WHEN MY COUSINS AND I WOULD LIE BACK ON
THE LAWN CHAIRS AND LOOK UP AT THE STARS AT NIGHT

WHEN WE WOULD RIDE ON BACK OF TRUCKS AND FEEL THE WIND
BLOW THROUGH OUR HAIR

WHEN THERE WERE NO CELL PHONES AND WE HAD TO USE PHONE
BOOTHS

IT REMINDS ME OF FAMILIES HAVING CLEAN FUN, LIKE
SUMMERTIME COOKOUTS AND LOVING YOU

THERE ARE SO MANY REASONS WHY YOU COULD FALL IN LOVE WITH
THIS PLACE

THE NUMBER ONE REASON IS THAT IT REMINDS ME OF THE BACK IN
THE DAY

EE

<u>Growth</u>

There is growth in all lessons

Even though sometimes you don't ask for it or deserve it

At least you get something out of it

PROVERBS 3:5-6

EE

I AM SAVED

IN MY DARKEST HOURS

YOU BEEN THERE FOR ME

IF IT WASN'T FOR YOU

I COULD NOT SEE

YOU MADE ME WHOLE AGAIN

YOU GAVE ME VICTORY

NOW I AM FREE FOR ALL ETERNITY

MY SOUL IS SAVED AND I WILL BEHAVE

FOR IT'S MY PLEASURE TO BE THIS WAY

I MEAN WHAT MORE CAN I SAY

I FEEL SO LIBERATED BECAUSE I AM SAVED

EE

DONE WITH LOVE FOR NOW

YOU WHO IS CALLED LOVE

BEEN THERE WITH YOU TO MANY TIMES

I LOVE YOU, BUT DONE WITH YOU FOR NOW

I DON'T TRUST YOU ANYMORE

I'M AFRAID OF YOU

EVEN THOUGH I DESIRE YOU

I WAISTED TO MUCH TIME WITH YOU

I HAVE GIVEN YOU, ME

I LOVED YOU UNCONDITIONALLY

YOU ALWAYS SEARCH FOR LOVE FROM SOMEONE ELSE

TO SUM IT UP, LOVE IS JUST NOT READY FOR ME BUT I WANT WAIT

I WILL LEAVE WITH ME PEACEFULLY

EE

I Am a Flower

2/22/2018

The array of assorted beautiful flowers, so many colors, and so many to love. Some bloom in the spring, summer, fall, and winter. Most are rare and none like the other. All have different smells and colors. They're not meant for just one occasion. Flowers are meant for showing love, and expression of how you want others to feel. Flowers make the room smile like the summertime. Flowers make transitions feels there's a Heaven above. Flowers make sick ones feel like they are loved. Flowers are more precious than most give credit. I was blessed to be called a flower as a baby. My grandmother called me Rosebud. Not quite a rose yet. I am beautiful, youthful, and heart innocent of love. Even was named Tinklebell because I stayed on my toes. I reminded my Ma of a flower she nurtured and mold. She loved on me like I was her own, I was sent by God and she loved me to the bone. I am blessed to be called a flower. I make others happy even when it showers.

EE

Stuck To Fly

I'm stuck in this bottle like the little boat sits. Wondering how did I get in here. How did I fit? As you sit back and look at it, like how in the world did she fit in it. Such as a baby stuck in its Mothers belly, that can't get out or shout. Please help me out. The Lord told you to release me out into the sea, maybe because you were not meant for me. I'm holding my breath, surrounded by water that I cannot swallow. You let me go and let the wind blow. I'm blown in the wind, about to lose my soul. My halo has a glow, who keeps me in control. This uncooked egg inside of this shell, it's obvious we are unequally yoked, as we can tell. We didn't gel to prevail or excel. You couldn't see the Angelic Earth Angel inside of me. Let me go flying away with my wings. You couldn't see my heart on the outside of me. How could this be when I wear my heart on my sleeves.

1 Corinthians 16:14

EE

<u>Even in Me</u>

Sweet birds fly towards the rainbow to seek Heaven's promise.

I feel the sweet whispers of winds blowing in my soul like the month of November when it's cold.

I see the high grass grow like it never seems to grow old.

Mountains standing tall for God with the courage of gold.

I respect the ocean waves roll, the mystery of how the peace carries the heavy loads.

I lay back and look up in the sky and mesmerize over the clouds that look like soft white pillows of snow.

I gaze at the blue skies that makes me happy and helps me grow.

The sweet satisfaction of God's creation that is explainable, who else could have created such magnificence. For some, it's hard to fathom.

I have experience his Heavenly presence, there is nothing this incredible of the essence of these Magical blessings.

I look and God is all around me in everything I see, even in me.

EE

WEAR IT WELL

HE SAYS I WEAR IT WELL FOR ALL I'VE BEEN THROUGH

FOR IT'S HARD TO TELL I'VE BEEN THROUGH SO MUCH

I STAY IN TOUCH WITH LIFE IN SPITE OF THE PAIN AND STRIFE

FOR IF THEY ONLY KNEW IT WOULD GIVE SOME THE BLUES

WHO WOULD THEY TURN TO

LIFE HAVE TRIALS, TRIBULATIONS, AND TEST

MAKE THEM ALL A TESTIMONY TO HELP SOMEONE ELSE

LIFES TO SHORT TO MARINATE ON THINGS YOU CAN NOT CHANGE

PEACE IS THE KEY, LOVE YOURSELF, AND KEEP GOD FIRST IN ALL YOU
DO

WEAR IT WELL YOU WILL PREVAIL

EE

SUBMISSIVE TO YOU

IM DONE WITH DYING OVER YOU

KILLING MY INNER BEING OVER YOU

FOR SOMETHING THAT'S THROUGH

I AM ALIVE AND AWAKE

READY TO SPREAD MY WINGS LIKE NEVER BEFORE

READY TO WALK THROUGH THOSE OPEN DOORS

SAVING MYSELF TO EXPLORE SOMETHING NEW

SUMMITING TO YOU AND ONLY YOU

FOR IM DONE AND THROUGH WITH ALL OF YOU

IF YOU WANT ME, YOU WILL WAIT AND NOT FAINT

ARE YOU UP FOR THE CHALLENGE, FOR FOREVER

EE

CLEANSE

AS I SUBMERGE DOWN INTO THIS WARM TYPE OF BLESSINGS

LOVING LAVENDER, THE SMELLS OF CITRUS SLICES OF ORANGES,
FRESH CUT ROSE JUST TO NAME A FEW.

LETTING GO OF THE OLD AND BRINGING IN THE NEW,

ALL TO BE ONE WITH YOU

HAVE THE FRANKINCENSE, SAGE, AND CANDLES BURNING

CLEANSING ME ON THE OUTSIDE AND WITHIN

BEING ONE WITH ME, TO BE FREE FROM THE DEBRIS

EE

FORBIDDEN FRUIT

IT SEEMS AS THOUGH YOU ARE THE FORBIDDEN FRUIT FOR MY SOUL

I WANT BITE, BUT YOU ARE BAD FOR MY DOME

YOU WILL CAUSE ME NOT TO BE WHOLE

WILL YOU WAIT FOR ME; TO BE MY KING

DO YOU KNOW YOUR ROLE LIKE THE MEN OF THE OLD

ASK MY SPIRITUAL FATHER FOR MY HAND

DON'T BE THE FORBIDDEN FRUIT BE, "MY MAN"

EE

A New Book and New Story

People have the right to change their mind

Even if they are blind

You can't make a person want or love you

You have to say love it or leave you

Open the door, walk out, and into another one as the new you

Be hurt but be threw

Stand at the door and wait for what God has for you

Close the book and write a another one about you

A new book and new story

Of tells of the Masters glory

You are the Author of your own life

No more books about pain or strife

Write the story that will allow your mind to become elevated

That will later blow their minds and centigrade it

Make them want to read your new story, of your victory and celebratory

EE

LET GO AND GROW

GRIEIVING SEEMS IT WILL LAST A LIFETIME

IM DONE WITH LOVE

LIVING IN THIS ATMOSPHERE WITH YOU IN DEAD SILENCE

THE ENERGY OF AWKWARDNESS

WAITING FOR THE DAY FOR US TO SEPARATE FROM THIS DRY SPELL

HURT IN MY HEART EACH TIME WE SAY SEE YOU LATER

WHERE DID THE LOVE GO

WHO KNOWS, I KNOW IT'S TIME TO LET GO AND GROW

FAREWELL LOVE SEE YOU AGAIN SOMEDAY

EE

MY KING

BEAT ON YOUR CHEST LIKE KONGO

YOU ARE THE KING OF THE JUNGLE

SHOW ME YOU'RE MY KING, POWERFULL AND STRONG

THE ESSENCE OF YOUR PRESENCE

YOU DON'T STRING OTHERS A LONG

YOU ARE CONFIDENT IN YOUR ANOINTING

OUT THERE DOING GOD'S WORK

IN YOUR ZONE, SHOWING ME YOU POSSESS A THROWN

RIGHT HERE IS WHERE YOU BELONG

RIDE WITH ME UNTIL THE END

REMOVE ALL THE DISTRACTIONS

PROTECT MY HEART FROM ALL HURT AND PAIN

LOVE ME WITH ALL YOUR HEART INTO THE TOMORROWS

HAPPINESS BUT TODAY IT IS GAIN

EE

I AM LOVE

MY FORTUNE IS MY HEART WITHOUT IT IM NOT WEALTHY

I GIVE UNSELFISHLY, EXPECTING ONLY THANK YOU IN RETURN

I RECEIVE KNOWING ONLY THIS IS GODS BLESSINGS GIVING
THANKSGIVING AND HAVING UNDERSTANDING OF HIS LESSONS

I AM LOVE, FOR IT SHINES, WITHIN ME LIKE THE DIAMOND FROM THE
RICHES PARTS OF THE WORLD

GOD TAUGHT ME HOW TO LOVE FOR THIS IS MY WEALTH AND MY
HEART IS MY MOTHERS PEARL

EE

NO LONGER DEFERRED

SUNRISE IN MY HEART AS IT AWAKES MY SOUL

STARTING TO FILL WHOLE TO CONTINUE TO GIVE MY HEART OF GOLD

WIND BLOWS AWAY MY SORROWS OFF INTO THE AIR NEVER TO
RETURN

TIME TO AWAKE AND HAVE SOME FUN IN THE SUN

AS I GO WHERE THE WIND BLOWS AND KEEP MY EYES ON THE
BEHOLDER

LIFE IS TO EXCELLENT TO CRY ON ANYONE SHOULDERS

IM READY TO LIVE, BE FREE, AND ALLOW THE GOD IN ME TO WATER
AND NURTURE THIS LOVELY TREE

HAVE SO MUCH FRUIT TO PRODUCE, TO GIVE, AND PLANT SEEDS ALL
OVER THE WORLD

GRANT YOU WISDOM FROM THESE LIFE EXPERIENCES THAT HAS
OCCURRED

IM GOING TO GIVE YOU ME, THE SOUL HERB

IN THIS LIFE THAT ALLOWS PEOPLE TO PLAY GAMES

THESE DECK OF CARDS THAT LIFE HAS DEALT

LIKE PROVERBS 13:12 OF HOPE DEFERRED

EE

Flying Free

I want to fly and glide; like a bird with my wings spread wide

Without a care in the world

Feeling life's natural high, with all the truth in the world that will set me free

The confessions of my soul will land me on my feet

Free from flying with baggage and weights on my shoulders

Me feeling free, with joy boiling over

EE

I AM A FAITH LEAPER

EVEN IF YOU WON'T KNOW WHAT THE FUTURE HOLDS, TAKE A LEAP AND SEE WHERE IT GOES...

BE A FAITH LEAPER

EE

HOW SWEET IT IS

LET THE OIL FLOW LIKE THE WATERS OF THE RIVERS

FLOWING OVER INTO MY SOUL

*SWEET LIVING WATER COMING INTO FRUITION OF THE BLESSINGS HE
HAS GIVEN THAT MAKES ME WHOLE*

*I EMBRACE THE SMALLEST NOTES OF THE WRITTEN LIFE'S BOOK OF
OLD*

THAT PROVIDES WISDOM FOR MY DESPERATE SOUL

WATCH ME GROW AND FLY HIGH OFF OF HIS AMAZING JOY

EE

_L'S_

LIFE LAST LONGER WHEN YOU LOVE FOR A LONG TIME

LIVE FOR LONGEVITY AND LAUGH BECAUSE IT'S A BEAUTIFUL
LUXURY

EE

LOVE BEYOND THE FLESH

I CAN'T WAIT UNTIL THE POINT WHEN YOU'RE ALL OVER MY LIPS

I CAN'T WAIT UNTIL YOUR HANDS ARE MOLDING MY HIPS

LOVING ON ME AS THOUGH I WAS YOUR LAST WOMAN

TAKING THIS RELATIONSHIP SLOW; NOT CARING ABOUT GOING FAST

EMBRACING THE MAGICAL MOMENTS

LET ME SEE YOUR HEARTBEAT

MAKING REAL LOVE WITH EVERY OUNCE OF ME

PAINT IT AND MAKE A LOVE MASTERPIECE

GIVE ME ALL YOU HAVE, SHOW YOUR INNER LOVE BEAST

BEYOND YOUR FLESH; GIVE ME YOUR MENTAL STIMULATION

SHOW ME BEYOND WORDS WITH TRUTHFUL CONVERSATIONS

SHOW ME YOUR WORLD TO THE POINT THERE IS AN UNDERSTANDING

RESPECT MY HEART AS IF YOU'RE A CONTRACT WITH ALL THE
ARRANGEMENTS

LOVE ME LIKE YOU HAVE NEVER LOVED ANY OTHER

MAKE ME YOUR WIFE NOT YOUR MOTHER NOR YOUR DAUGHTER

I HAVE YOU AS MY KING, YOU WILL BE MY FIRST PRIORITY WITH GODS PERMISSION THERE IS NO ARGUING

LET'S MAKE LOVE DIFFERENTLY AND BEFORE THE FLESH HAVE ANY INVOLVEMENT

LET'S START THIS NEW THING IN LOVE AND MAKE THAT OUR PRIORITY

EE

I Must Admit I'm Drawn to You

Part 1

The presence of your smile makes me proud

As you speak to the people, it's no doubt your words reach hearts abound

Wrapped up in your intelligence fills my soul, with melodies' lyrically I'm going to let it be

Out of my element of my energy, but I can put the words I'm rhyming with this poetry

I'm drawn to your words and teachings of our history

Giving me joy looking in your eyes of the windows of your soul, your dopiness encourages me to be bold

You give power to the people

For your soul is old, you inherited a heart of gold

You're a divine King and your covering for a Woman is no question; it can't be denied

I love all of you; that God-fearing spiritual evolution about you

You're not a common Man, but your name no doubt fits you

I must admit I'm drawn to you

EE

I Must Admit I'm Drawn to You

Part 2

Waking up at 2 am writing poetry about a celebrity is giving me life in this Floetry

I couldn't let it be, this one brings out the best in me

I can keep flowing on this paper, like this page will never end

I had more to say about you, so I split the poem into two

You have so much to give and I could learn more from you

I'm a holey sponge that doesn't want to be squeezed

I want to soak up all that holy water and let it immerse inside of me

Your words so purified why even bother just keep me in the water

I want to drink from you, for it would give me a life longevity even if it's for just a few

You're like a fountain of youth on display, I want to drink of you if I may

You're like an attractive book, I want to pull off of the shelf

You make me want to read because your knowledge is wealth

You're rich in your soul, you bring such good health

You can't help how God created you, no need to boast

You're the start of something that makes me want to create more

I'm drawn to you, there is no question

It's the knowledge in you, I want to rest in

EE

LIVE

EVERYTHING IN LIFE LIVES TO DIE

ALLOW A LITTLE BIT OF YOURSELF AT A TIME TO DIE TO LIVE FOR
ETERNITY

EE

The Elders Love

I walk through life seeing you through the windows of my soul

Admiring you no matter your race with this pure heart of gold

I see you in the winter time like I'm looking through a Christmas snow globe

The way you hold hands like love never grows old

As I pass by you two sitting on a bench of old, no age can define your every lasting life molds

As you walk the beach embracing the waters, I know you have washed away your many sorrows

You have been through time that is never so promising, but you don't watch the time of life you only embrace for tomorrows

You have prepared for the life, so you can see better days

I see in your Queens' eyes there's no worries it has all been paid

When I see you out in the yard or in the garden, you know there is a harvest of love and you're never starving

When I see you out on the dance floor still cutting a rug, you know that life has balance and you both are still both in love

As I walk through restaurants and I see you on your date, it gives me a sight of the love life of promises and I cannot wait

My days of working in the hospital field seeing each other at the bedside say this love you have is real and you do not hide

Even at the very end of time your love still goes on, on the other side

For they seem they cannot live without each other even at the beginning of time

For when one transition on I'm sure they ask God to let the other inside

I have a place for you right beside me my dear, my wife or husband, lover, and best friend

In this unbelievable place called Heaven, you're going to love it here

I wish you could come and join me, honey, I don't want you to be a long in fear

For we are one flesh and you will always have me near

I will be waiting when it's time for God to bring you home

He still has big plans for us to unwind and embrace these thrones

EE

Bee Filled with Honey

Never trust a Man with only words, those sweet whispers of nothing which we all have heard.

Never trust a Man with so much to give, but never any time. You'll be starting over with nothing left, not even a dime.

Never trust a Man who is bound in his religion, but a Man with a spiritual relationship and you see all God have given.

Never trust a Man who doesn't honor his Mother, he will only treat you bad like all of his Fathers.

Never trust a Man who is only after your body, for with his plan he will only bring your sorrows.

Never trust a Man for how he looks, he will be looking in the mirror more than the hour you took.

Never trust a Man who only comes out at night, for all he wants is sex then leave you with an appetite.

Never trust a Man who only text when he's at home, you know what time it is you just leave him alone.

Only trust yourself for you are God's Woman, he will give you what you need a bee filled with honey.

In life you only feed honey to these colletidea bees, wait on the nectar from the Lord, he will give you what you need.

For he will supply all your needs, even filled those voids of desires you feed

So don't get caught in these hives, chased by all types of bees or you end up with a surprise, you see...

EE

Again

I Remember I was single for years and now I'm back at that same exact place again.

Left with feelings of nothing, but starting over with the same face.

Time for that feeling of contentment to rise back up again.

Thank God for my friends who have by back, oh how I love them.

Never can get past a point with men, kind of like stunted hair growth under your chin.

You will find out they are unequally yoked and end up being one of your friends.

I want to say unfortunately, I was taught to forgive. When you forgive it allows you the freedom to live.

You can't question God's work, you only move forward, or be stuck in a place that will have you feeling short lived.

And thank God that it happened, he saved you from some horrid episode that could have turned into a Netflix original, that all ends up like comedy central.

I know we ask God, Lord what did I do? You did nothing wrong in this season, it just wasn't for you.

I have plans to teach him and teach you too. To put ME first in everything that you do.

Hang on my child you know I got you, I've been there since the beginning and I will see you through.

No need to worry about the financial things, I will supply all you needs for I am your true King.

No Man is ready so, I removed him with ease, so don't worry yourself I have your back true Queen.

That is without a doubt that is only facts, you will be redeemed.

I only say "well" hallelujah anyhow because in the end you will laugh at it all and thank God for these learning falls.

To get back up and rise, my friend isn't it a blessing to have God to mend your heart again.

EE

The Presence of God

Smile like the sun in the spring to make someone day

Be the waves of calmness to give peace when someone can't get away

Be the star in someone eyes when they need to feel loved

Be a moon to help someone see in the darkness of life

Be the shade like the trees when someone is in the heat of their days

Shelter others from the storms to keep them from harm's way

Be the refreshing mist on a gloomy day to ensure they will be ok

Be the hello like the wind on a crisp cold winter's day

Plant the seed of kindness, so love can grow in their hearts to past along the amazing presence of God

EE

Simply Beautiful

A man once told me if a Man would only listen, he would learn a lot from you. You're wise as an old oak tree and wise enough to receive the worst news. A leader by divine order in the darkest regime. He would skip games and make life easier to go through. He would find true love and his heart would rest in the love of the bayou. He could take a deep breath, with ease and just love you. For it is not hard to love you for you put a stamp on everyone's hearts that meet you. For you're just simply beautiful...

EE

Blessed with Melanin

Hello Sun, come and give me some of that Vitamin D that's good for me

Good for my Melanin Tree

Body so rich it makes its own oils

So rich it smell sweet through my salivated pores

Skin so soft, make you want to grab at it

Look so good, it make others mad at it

It's something about those array Melanin colors

Always the topic of conversation cause everybody "adores" it

I can't help I've been blessed with such a beautiful color

I love being black for there are reasons for it

EE

Come Home Baby

I feel as though my words are lost and alone

A little piece of my spirit and soul is gone

Left empty without a song

This life won't leave me alone

I feel love pulling on me, telling me to come home

Drawn to me like a bee to a honeycomb

Gravitated by my alluring beauty, like a tasty meal

Giving me energy that I need to feel, which is apparently real

While you're loving my zest and cultivated by my zeal

I sense you want to help my majestic broken heart heal

Life has the possibilities of love and a friendship to permanently congeal

I feel your spirit saying come home baby my love for you is real

EE

Hex

I should have never told her I was in love with you

Afterwards, it was like she had a strong hold on you

Our relationship died like old leaves in a tree when the skies are no longer blue

You not loving me, me not loving me, but me loving you

I had to flee from all the mental debris

From the Hex that was put on me

Washed clean from the evil of she and the D…

So long live the Queen

No more soul ties holding on to me

My Majesty released me, I decree and rebuking that energy from inside of me

God will fight all your battles even the ones you cannot see

Daily meditating on the Psalms chapter 27 and 35 allowing it to permeate in me

There are spiritual warfare's going on, be mindful of who you allow in your life or else you will end up in a war zone

You'll end up dying a firing death like the ozone

Keep your mind and heart protected, those are gemstones

Keep your armor of God on and stay in Gods zone

_EE_

Broken Vegetarian

It's hard being in a place where it feels you're not wanted, desired, or needed

Grieving is like eight-day-old leftovers that's spoiled, screaming don't eat it

Like once delicious bread, now old, molded, and fuzzy on the edge

Life feels like bad food that has made me sick, taking half of my soul from lovely to gluttony

Some days I feel like going, some days I don't

I'm all in my head, I'm up in this bed and dairy-free ice cream is all I want

I feel like a pot of my brother's seasoned chicken feet

I just want to stay home and cry and eat

This miserable love has me sick like an old batch of meat

This has to stop, I can't take it anymore

I wish I could eat it all and walk right out the door

This bad service has me mad and nervous

I believed I was going to get the best of this loving service

I'm trying to make the best out of this situation

I'm craving some victory, instead of frustration

It has me going crazy, why did this have to happen to me

But now I'm starting to feel hungry

I don't know where to go, but I can taste my destiny

Writing this poem has my appetite open like a delicious recipe

I am ready to be release and be free to eat a different kind of meat

Bring Forth

Have what you want

Manifest your dreams through your eyes

Visualize what you want you'll be surprised

Meditate on your future and watch it come alive

Plant your seeds to create a harvest

And watch the universe grow what you need

You have the power to bring forth what you believe

You have to put in work and bring your best

Keep working on and watch your life be blessed

EE

Our True Love

He calls me sunshine

I call him my moon

I'll be his ocean

He'll be my earth boom

We'll flow by the river

We'll relax by the pond

We'll walk with God's creatures and welcome with open arms

We'll live off the land

We'll live by the fruit

We'll indulge in the nectar

We are planted by the root

We are strong in our love

We are powerful in our youth

This love that we are given is the reflection of you

EE

For Heaven is Success

Weeks passing by like minutes

Minutes passing by like seconds

Time waits for no one, but we are still creatures of habit

Lost in the daily, day to day that no longer awaits

Not taking the time out to embrace the seconds of the day

Challenging obstacles, devasting news, but still, we must roll on we have to pay those dues

Unapologetically behavior, unapologetically blues

All that life has to offer, it leaves you little clues

Clear your head, the Master that controls everything

Get away from the day to day to see what Heaven brings

Capture each moment, as if it's your last

Make all moments count, life is more than just a blast

Be with people you love and allow them to love on you

We only have one life and that's unapologetically too

Make it all good, and make it all count

It's only one way to Heaven and that's the Jesus route

Don't let this life pass you by without living life

Asking the Father to let you in with the other souls who made it in right

No one is perfect, for there was only one and that's the son of God

You wasn't put on God's green Earth to give up after coming this far

No more hesitating strive with the best

Yes there will always be obstacles and the most challenging test

Continue to live close to right and do your best

You got this, for Heaven is the ultimate success

EE

Sand, Ocean, Sun

To walk on me, you are walking on Mans history

Plant your feet and walk on top of footprints of many

Lay down with me, share your stories, or think of talents to birth

You are strong Kings and Queens on this God-given earth

Plans for hopes and dreams of tomorrows being overly rehearsed

Kids come to build your dreams made out of sands castles

Be sure to realize you are God's true ordained masters

Get lost in my waves for I am Gods healing green and blue waters

Close your eyes, come and lay on me, I will take your mind off your sorrows

Leave it all here, with God in charge no need to have any fears

For like God I will never leave nor forsake you, I will always be here

I am sand a reminder of Gods everlasting love, you are in his hands

Come, get your blessed healing from us, we are God amazing creations

Embrace me the sand as you emerge in this sunbeam of greatness

Let us hug on you to feel as if you've already won and life is now weightless

Leave in peace and come back again someday

I'll be waiting in this peaceful sun, I will always invite you to stay

EE

Off Track

Master, please forgive me for my lies and my truths

I've been disobedient which have caused me to be misused

I've done it to myself and there is no excuse

For you have taught me well there is no reason for this fool

I will do better I'm just asking you to hold my hand

I need your guidance for this life it is such a demand

I fight to live right each and every day

For this is a lifestyle that cannot be unapologetically changed

You have to follow the passage of the word that cannot be rearranged

Even though it can be hard, from the day to day temptations

To separate yourself from the wolf perpetrating to love you

Time to go into mediation to hear from you

Time to go into prayer to fight the accused

I am ready again God, I am back on track

Sometimes I fall short but no one is perfect

I'm asking for forgiveness and pushing to be a fervent servant

EE

Heaven's Voice

As the wind blows over my shoulders, I feel my little hairs move

How could this be

Wind so strong I feel my little hairs move on beat

Laying on the back patio with a good book in my hand

Reading a few chapters, mental stimulation is always the plan

With that mind mediation playing softly in my ears

Hearing the water fountain spouting sounds that's so tranquil

Embracing the breeze that blows in my ears

I feel so elevated that God's presence has to be near

This is the life, I must be totally sincere

It doesn't take much to please me, I'm just keeping it real

But this right here is beyond a gift of His living will

Thank you for this feeling for it is so amazingly real

To hear the voice of Heaven as I lay here and chill

EE

Just Watch and Listen

Birds sucking the nectar out of the sweetest flowers

Going back and forth within the hour

Getting his and her nectar for the day

As I watch them play and then fly away

Listening to the melodies of Sade in the midday on a Thursday

Laying out and writing poems while I sunbathe

As I close my eyes and she takes me to different places

She calms my spirit even through life phases

She soothes my soul and gives me elevation

This is living the life of satisfaction

EE

Pray, Eat, Drink, and Be Merry

All my family loves does is pray, eat, drink, and be merry

Dance the night way drunk with family matters

Hidden secrets but no love lost, we still all together at all cost

As I watch the time pass with the throwback of shots and laughter

No one going anywhere, in this life any faster

Some have truly set many examples

Some too lazy to follow it afterward

Miss understandings and miscommunications

You overheard that one of them caught the vipers

Stress on high, but still will indulge in a piece of the pie

Life to good you may as well eat a piece of rye

No navigations needed they all are in the same city

Take life slow there's nowhere else to go, for some life pity

Smells of fried foods and cigarette smoke

Fill the room up with food and choke

Love runs deep you can tell by the kiss on the cheeks

No matter the circumstances, we keep bail on fleek

Most of the Men in our family are hard to reach

Not sure what happened to them, they let the demons have them beat

Maybe because there are no male examples

Maybe because they never experience that life on campus

But we are a hardworking family at least some of us, who only serve one Master

We pray, eat, drink, and be merry and that's how life goes in most family...

EE

Tangible Things

I love tangible things

It makes me feel good at the joy that it brings

Like going to the store when your favor artist album drop

Like stopping at the bookstore to pick up that brand new stock

Of a new title that peeks your interest

Or one you have been waiting on that seems like you been waiting on for centuries

Or that new DVD that you just have to have

The movie was so good, you will pay the cash

And what about that soundtrack that you had to get real fast

Before it all sell out, you want to be the first in line

For that new game that your parents just dropped a dime

This is the last game you get when you know you'll get another

I have to have things I can touch

You cherish them because you can feel and it won't disappear

Unless you lose but again these are only things

Life is more than replaceable means

EE

I Got You

Days when I feel my heart and soul crumbling, I look to God to mend my broken heart and my mind from wondering.

Days when I feel drained, all I can do is ask God for help to get me through. For life can be a myth that's pass truth.

Days when I feel like I don't know where I'm going, I ask God to direct me. I know I'm moving slow instead of running.

Days when I feel afraid and don't what to do, I ask my Father to protect me. I know that he will get me through.

One of the reasons I have so much faith in you, I remember you saying I got you.

EE

<u>Not Worth It</u>

Many have come and gone

With the same old deniable love song

You're the one I shouldn't have let go

When you left, you took a piece of my soul

Honestly, I miss what I deserve but not worth the hustle of beefy hurbs

You are only united soul ties that still want to stay around me to get high

I realize I'm like Hawaii, I am Paradise

I want to stay far from you and all your lies

If I got in it, I can get out of it

I'll figure life out and bounce

EE

Empty Seed

Betrayal, jealousy, throw shaders, conniving haters, milking your dopiness, stepping on toes, to try and make you lose focus, trying to still your glow, she so hopeless. The ones who are hoes getters, with the wrinkle in their nose sniffers, no style and it shows by the picking of your clothes, snooty as you want to be, selfish as you're gonna be, in the workplace acting all uppity. This is what you choose to be, but you don't gotta be. You went to school, you still have a soul you see. We don't have nothing to lose but our royalty. Honestly, I have no use for thee, you're not my cup of tea. You're just an empty seed...

EE

Let's Celebrate

You don't need a reason to celebrate. Be the reason to celebrate. Celebrate Yourself.

EE

<u>I Am Falling Particles</u>

When I open the window and the sunlight beams shine through, I see those little particles floating around

As I watch them fall, I think "thank you God for allowing me to see life for what it is"

Thank you for opening up my eyes to even the smallest things in life

Thank you for refining me as a gem

Thank you for another transition in my spirituality

Thank you for another change in my being

Forgive me for my known and unknown sins

Mend and purify my broken limbs

Allow them to grow and bare sweeter fruit on them

Thank you for allowing me to see the falling particles

For I am pieces of falling particles, that needs to fall into your loving hands to make me a better Woman

EE

Control Your Focus

At some point you have to stop hurting so you can focus on change

You can't focus on things you can't change

But the things you can change, focus on that point of no return on changing the game

Focus on rearranging your mental capacity

Controlling your life it's yours and yours only

No man has demesne over you

A bare finger is an open window for the rib to be seen without skin straight to the heart that belongs only to God

Focus on changing the game making band tans on the beach with your King

Until then be complete, be whole, be the beloved of the Creators

He gave you the gift of life so what more can you ask for

One author told me to enjoy one moment at time, and transform stones into stepping stones, for this is the pathway to peace, presence, and prosperity

For this is my focus and my prayer over and over again...

EE

I Am Beautiful Inside Out

Out here natural with no makeup

Yes I'm flawed in the mornings when I wake up

Flaws on fleek, God made me

Nothing defines me but GOD who designed me

Smelling good that will make you want to stay up

Smelling like a liquid coconut

Smelling like sweet butter cups

When beauty is a factor for some but not for you

Some say I'm more beautiful in person

I say what you see is what you get

Face, body, and that heavenly scent

EE

Done Talking

As I enter the city of dry bones

The drained energy of nothingness

Haunting your soul like a dirty peasants mess

I watch your big hearts make us all suffer for all the gossip and unthoughtful murmurs

I can't expect anyone to understand me

There's only a million in one who gets me

No more trying to pry open cracks and mended floorboards

It is time to move ahead and cast my own anchors

For no one is listening, it doesn't really matter

Knowledge has been out of love, forget the ongoing chatter

I've been an outcast to some since I was born

Not excepting the reward of my love in return

But now, I have thrown the towel in

It has never been a game, I want all of us to win

EE

I Want To Be Free At the Top

My imaginations are like the algae at the bottom of the ocean that breaks away and floats to the top releasing itself to the surface to find a place to be somewhere different

EE

Just Feel It, Feel It, Feel It

Dance your pain away

Dance the night until day

Do it because the beat fills your soul

Allow it to make you feel whole

Dance to sweat and purify that load

Let it bless your dome

Dance to make your food taste homegrown

Dance to fill your house with the essence of magical moments

Dance until it takes you places you want to feel romance

Let the music change your life

It feel so good makes you get so hype

JUST FEEL IT, FEEL IT, FEEL IT

Close your eyes and feel the beat in your bones

Let the beat take your body in your zone

Like there is no one else in the room

Let it make you want to experience the inevitable chemistry of two bound like love clones

Make you want to bring him home

It makes your heart beat with laughter and love made to bloom

Let it make you get out your seat to the dance floor because you can't take it anymore

Let the beat make you bob your heads

Let your bootie move from right to left, up and down and round and round

Whine your body to the sound of the beats

Move your legs to the rhythm, make him say come here girl and get on your feet

Dance in the daytime, midday, night time, all the time

JUST FEEL IT, FEEL IT, FEEL IT

EE

My Loving Angels

One day I fell asleep, but you woke me by the pulling of my feet.

When I woke I didn't see anyone around, but what I found was smoke.

Smoke from the kitchen of the boiled eggs, I left on the stove.

I didn't know that I drifted off in a zone, but no one was home

I was home alone. I realize it was one of my Guardian Angels watching over me.

I am blessed even if I can't see thee.

Thank you for saving my life more than twice.

One day I want to be like you.

Where I can pray, protect, and bring back what is needed to meet the needs of others.

Thank you, for all you have done for me, surrounding me, and keeping me.

Thank you, God, for allowing your loving Angel assigned to me to guard me always.

EE

<u>*You Are Not the One*</u>

I smell the familiar smell that I knew too well

What happened to your smell that magnetic smell that I craved like hell

When you were gone I would try to find your smell in the scent of your clothes

Sleeping in those sheets holding your pillow because I missed you

Now the new familiar smell has taken over

Now yours is gone away, it only lingers when I'm not sober

The walls are closing in on me and what I can I say

It's killing me inside so I cannot stay

I hate it and you denied it

When you love someone even their smell becomes a part of you

When their smell is gone it gives you the blues

It's like the wind blew it away like Heaven knew

You're familiar smell was only a sign that you weren't mine and that's fine

EE

Watch God's Show Unfold

There is a reason for it all

In the most horrific falls in life

Doing what needs to be done and waiting on what's to come

All sorts of obstacles coming my way not much for some

Most people think I'm on a run

Healing and maintaining the mind, not for fun

Looking forward and pushing to not press the past memory of reruns

Not making more bad episodes with the old that's not worth a pot of gold

Set up for failure and not to win, life will only repeat itself again

I'm pressing forward to see what God has for me

No repeated shows or rehearsals

Watch life unfold universal

It has a way of working out

I'll put God first and let him sort it out

EE

Guard Your Heart

My glass and woven heart life

Shattered pieces by people

Dropping to the ground

Picking pieces back up again and again

Cutting myself, dripping blood from my healing hands

Making sacrifices from my bleeding heart

In certain seasons it breaks

I find the shape that it's in and put it back together again

My heart threaded on the inside of my flesh

Piece by piece unwoven because everyone takes a piece of it

I take it back and sew it back to my flesh again

I ask myself is being too loving a sin

PROVERBS 4:23

EE

Talk To Me, I Will Talk to You

I'm waiting and anticipating

What to do

I'm through

I'm waiting on answers from you

Please talk to me

I don't see anything

I'm not sure what to do

Can you help me through

I need you

I'm talking all in my head

Get on your knees and talk to me, I will talk to you

EE

Queenship

Of course, he gave me life back, removed the old pain that manifested rain

I feel me in my Father's arms, holding, comforting, and keeping me strong

I am his beloved daughter, heir to the Throne

All this mess will leave me alone

As I sing sweet melodies of love songs

From hearing the beats of my own heart now

Made new, crowned, and enthrone

Sitting Queenship in the cool

Dripping jewels in the nude

Naked like Eve, I'm so pure

Standing strong, righteous and secured

I am a Goddess that shall not want

I am entitled, look where I come from

It's well-deserved I have been patient

Serving you like a beat down waitress

I still have a lot to learn and still aim to win

I have to immerse in the word and mend it in my heart

Until then sitting on the Thrown is where I will start

EE

<u>So Us</u>

I place my head on your masculine chest

Falling asleep to your heartbeat

Thank you, baby, for letting me under your wing

Thank you for loving me with all my flaws while watching me while I sleep

Close your eyes and go with me

You make me want to immerse my body in the deep ocean with you and not feel afraid

Sink our toes in the warm sands of exotic islands

I want to watch the stars as they wink at us

Marinate in our kisses and be one with each other

Watching the sunset at the end of the days

Like how gators are amazed by the Everglades

Chilling in the midday in the shade

Like the fish embracing the beauty of the waves at the end of the day

Laying listening to the sweet melodies of Sade

I can't believe with both feel this way

Getting lost in love but don't get scared then fly away

Like the beautiful birds who lost their way

EE

Still Prayers for You

I have thoughts, glimpses, and visions of you

I see your smile shining through my mind

The laughter in your eyes that created happiness in the room

You graced us with small enchanted moments by you

Saved text messages and voicemails I still have from you

Need a part of you to still be here

A few more months and I would have seen you

Soul snatched too soon with so much left to do

Taking to soon by the pulling of a gun of the boy in blue

Now left in the news with nothing I can do, but have moments of the blues

When life starts for some it's gone and we have no clue this would happen to you

You asked me to send prayers up for you

And of course that I will do

Even with the end of time, I still will do

May you rest in Paradise and know that I love you

EE

You Are the Author

It never starts like it begins

Like a good book, the beginning never is the ending

Take life for what it is

Take the time to write each page how you like it

Don't expect the pages to be how you started to write them

Stories change all the time or you may want to rewrite them

Embrace the pages, write line by line

Take one moment at a time

Expecting a better chapter each phase of your life

Just finish what you started and add a little spice

New stories created and new books begin

You will lose some characters and some will audition for different roles

Whoever is worth the ride, take them on a memorable journey

This is your story, tell it how you like

Just don't give up, you're the author of your life

EE

Heartfelt Beats of Neo-Soul

As I sit and write these poems, lyrics, or rhymes

Whatever you want to call it

Know I'm sitting here lilt and zoned out without a doubt in my own lane

I won't complain

Listening to the dope beats of neo-soul

It makes me feel my soul is dope

I can't hold it in, these beats has me feeling like I'm going to win

I bob my head

Feeling myself, these sounds have to be good for your health

My heart is a rhythm of beats, so why wouldn't it seek for these beats

I advise the mothers to start from the womb

The satisfaction of the heart will groom the little you

For when the beats are felt in the heart it won't let us stray too far

It gets down in your soul and to their hearts

It keeps our love close and doesn't tear us apart

EE

Happy to be Amongst the Living

Sermons in the morning to start the day

God first, I mean what more can I say

God said he will provide all my needs

A pray first, oh yes indeed

Doing my part to please the Lord

Lord have mercy on my soul, it's not about rewards

I need to feel whole, righteous, and bold

I'm by no means perfect, I mean I live in a life that sometimes makes you feel worthless

But He said He will never leave me nor for sake me

I stand on uneven pavement

I will be a cheerful giver

I don't mind, life could end and would be my last whisper

Then you're gone and there are no more tomorrows

Only love ones unhappy with heartfelt sorrows

I'm only grateful to be amongst the living and see the richness that He has given

I'm not talking about money

But the halcyon days of life making it to good ole Sunday

EE

No End Season

When it is your time you will finish

You will start and you will finish

Just like they say you will know when they are the one

You don't want to wake up with anyone else in the morning

Sun peeking through the blinds

It's time to get up and pull from the heart

Every day is a new day to be great

Get up and start again and don't be late

Push forward and set a date

Be sure to participate don't miss out on anything

It is never too late

To create and be great

How I start my mornings while destiny awaits

I'm almost there, almost at the end

When I had the epiphany and the tears came in

I knew you were the one that had no end

This is my season to win

EE

Don't Live In Where You Come From

People say don't forget where you come from

I don't think you can ever forget, where you come from

But moving forward is not where you come from, it is in your past

Appreciate it for what it's worth and be steadfast

Reliving is what you will be doing

Killing the spirit trying to rebuild it

Nothing is worth settling for the masses

Be drawn to the future, for it's not what you're used to

You're not comfortable with it

Sip some good ole Russian tea, but don't live in

Leave it all behind, no need to rewind

Learn from it, but you can't sit in it

It's lost in seconds, gone in a day, and it's all yesterdays

Can't get that back as a matter of fact

As the mind get older that doesn't even last

Be a harbinger, it better in this season

For we need hopes for tomorrow

Living in the past can bring pain and sorrow

No turning back unless it's to give back for some ones else hope for tomorrows

EE

Million Dollar Worth

A Women's worth is more than the pulling up her skirt

The backlash from disrespectful words that hurt

Admire her Queenship and her own turf

As she admires her million dollar worth, that's under her skirt

Give and it shall be given unto you

Respect in the nude

Not flesh to flesh

But what's honest and true

Her heart that beats for you

EE

To Think

Sometimes complete silence is the best way to solve life mysteries

EE

He Died to Self

When he spoke and told me he died to self, I knew he knew the true meaning of God's good health and wealth

We all have to die to self, God will provide good health and wealth

Good health and wealth in our heart, mind, body, and spirit

We only have to move, be still, and listen

Move placing one foot in front of the other

Be still and know that He is God

And listen to his voice, even if it is only one word

And place no one above him

To die to self is to live in God's good health and wealth

EE

Pastiche

I use to feel like the lissome Mary, there was just something about me, Lagniappe

Every day I carry a little bit of the glamourous Bradshaw, dalliance relationships, but ebullience in my writing

Nowadays I feel like the becoming of Polly, no labels, only live one day at a time, without a care in the world, and that is just fine this is my demesne

In reality, I am how God made me, an opulent piece of Art with pyrrhic

EE

Nothing but Love Peoples

I love thoughtful people

I was just thinking of you people

The just because of people

The little tokens of love given people

The love own you and give you hugs type of people

Who display love in small ways people

Who simply adore you, type of people

Who love you to no end, type of people

I love you in spite of, type of people

I'm here for you no matter what, type of people

Those keep in touch, type of people

Who will always be there for you, type of people

Who will stand beside you, type of people

Those who come to break bread with you, type of people

Who welcome you into their home, type of people

Those make you feel at home, type of people

No judgment, type of people

Your business is your business, type of people

Those are my peoples

To know end peoples

And I am their people because I am those type of peoples

EE

Time to Clean My System

I see you out of my peripheral

My intuition on tap like only top shelf-liquor

Like an addict to crystal meth, you're trying to kill us

I'll blow up the lab, it will soon be revealed

If I can't trust you then I'll prepare the process to heal

Plans to attend rehab to move forth to live

The taste for you is gone and short-lived

Like coke on the table, that has them in a zone that leave them numb to the bone

I'm done with your love, your addition is all wrong

EE

I Am My Fix

I'm starting to feel radiant again

More moments of effervescent laughter

Coming alive efflorescence roses

With my gambol spirit that has awakened in my bones

An elixir of love in my soul

Such eloquence in my elisions

My felicity is where I rest

For this is incipient of how I truly supposed to feel

I am a Madam, I am my fix

EE

Rich Hips

This doesn't make any sense

These pants want fit

This makes me sick

Maybe I'm getting rich in my hips

These pants want zip

I looked the same size last year

What happens to the glimpse under my nips

I can't see myself anymore

Maybe it was all that fried food and Frenchie's

Time to get in the gym and work off these hinges

To find the denouement of where these rich hips came from

Small to some but looks nice to others

Nothing wrong with you girl, you look like your Mother

Out of know where, but I know where I came from

This soul food won't leave me alone

EE

Authentically You...

Who is that under that skin, authentically...

Reveal and let's see

Tell them to love it or leave you alone

Tell them, this is how God created me

This is how I suppose to be

Be free of your inside mystery

Take your coat off and embrace the cold

People will talk but let it go

At least you are authentically you

Hell, make them take off their shoes

Let them walk miles to pay your dues

You owe them nothing they're misused

God didn't make clones he made jewels

So just be authentically you

EE

BY ERYKA EDWARDS

DEDICATION

My poetry book is dedicated to my Mother, my Guardian Angel, Minnie Bell McCrae. She planted the seeds of salvation. Without her, I would not be the Woman that I am today. To Ms. Sharon "BYRD" Isaiah, who looked out for me as a kid. These two Women laid the foundation for creativity. They taught me how to entertain myself, live a life of peace, love, and happiness. And to my oldest Sister Mrs. Patricia Minter who inspired me to write again.

Made in United States
Orlando, FL
22 May 2025

61496642R00073